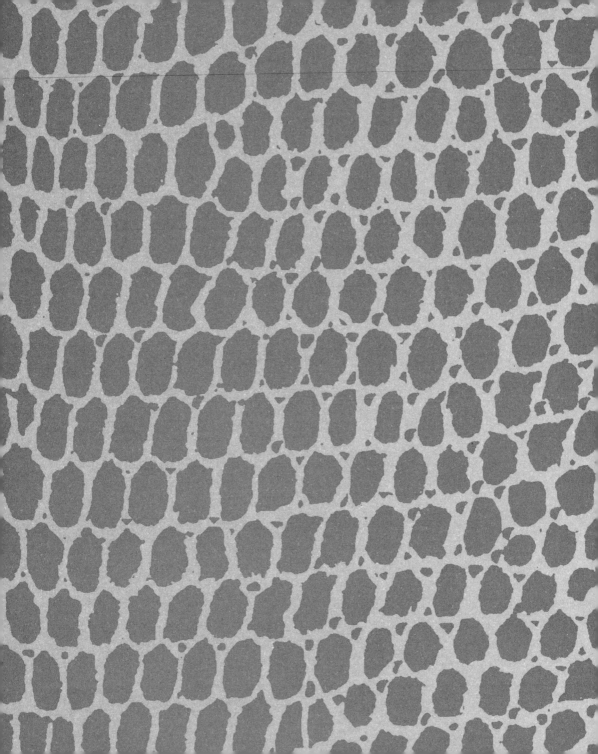

Aquarium
Care of
Bettas

DAVID E. BORUCHOWITZ

Aquarium Care of Bettas

Project Team
Editor: Brian M. Scott
Copy Editor: Mary Connell
Design: Laura J. Bongarzone
Series Design: Stephanie Krautheim & Leah Lococo Ltd.

T.F.H. Publications
President/CEO: Glen S. Axelrod
Executive Vice President: Mark E. Johnson
Publisher: Christopher T. Reggio
Production Manager: Kathy Bontz

T.F.H. Publications, Inc.
One TFH Plaza
Third and Union Avenues
Neptune City, NJ 07753

Discovery Communications, Inc. Book Development Team
Maureen Smith, Executive Vice President & General
  Manager, Animal Planet
Carol LeBlanc, Vice President, Marketing and Retail
  Development
Elizabeth Bakacs, Vice President, Creative Services
Peggy Ang, Director, Animal Planet Marketing
Caitlin Erb, Marketing Associate

Exterior design ©2006 Discovery Communications, Inc. Animal Planet, logo and Animusings are trademarks of Discovery Communications, Inc., used under license. All rights reserved. *animalplanet.com*

Interior design, text, and photos ©2006 T.F.H. Publications, Inc.

Printed and bound in China
06 07 08 09 10 1 3 5 7 9 8 6 4 2

Library of Congress Cataloging-in-Publication Data
Boruchowitz, David E.
Aquarium care of bettas / David E. Boruchowitz.
p. cm.
Includes index.
ISBN 0-7938-3763-4 (alk. paper)
1. Betta. I. Title.
SF458.B4B67 2006
639.3'77–dc22
2006013107

This book has been published with the intent to provide accurate and authoritative information in regard to the subject matter within. While every precaution has been taken in preparation of this book, the author and publisher expressly disclaim responsibility for any errors, omissions, or adverse effects arising from the use or application of the information contained herein. The techniques and suggestions are used at the reader's discretion and are not to be considered a substitute for veterinary care. If you suspect a medical problem consult your veterinarian.

The Leader In Responsible Animal Care For Over 50 Years!™

www.tfhpublications.com

Table of **Contents**

Introduction

Hobbyists all over the world keep and breed bettas for their beautiful colors and finnage, and that is the context in which most people are familiar with these fish. Many attributes that bettas exhibit make them ideal wet pets, but unfortunately other betta attributes have led hobbyists to mistreat many of them unintentionally. In this book you will learn how to properly care for these wonderful creatures.

Chapter 1

Why Do You Want to Keep a

Betta?

Buying any type of fish on impulse is usually not good for you or the fish. The decision to purchase a betta, like the decision to purchase any living thing, should be based on knowledge and planning. Nevertheless, many people will decide they want to keep a betta as a pet, and you may very well, too! So, what makes bettas so appealing?

Bettas Defined

The common betta is known to science as *Betta splendens*. The genus "*Betta*" is shared by many related species that are also sometimes called bettas. The Latin name "*splendens*" given to this particular species actually means "splendid"—a very good choice for this beautiful fish. An older name for this fish was "Siamese fighting fish," but most aquarists today use the generic name—betta—as a common name for the various ornamental strains of this species.

Most bettas are about 2.5 to 3 inches (7 cm) long, with females of the species being slightly smaller than males. Depending on the strain, the male's fins can be as long as the body. It is not really an exaggeration to

Betta or Beta?

You can pronounce scientific names any way you want. Most people pronounce this one as BET-tuh (similar to "better"). A good number, however, pronounce it as BAY-tuh (as for "beta"). The first pronunciation is closer to original Latin, and it avoids any confusion with the name of the second letter in the Greek alphabet, which is commonly used in mathematics and in software terminology.

Many of the male bettas that you'll find in pet shops have a body length of about 2 inches (5 cm).

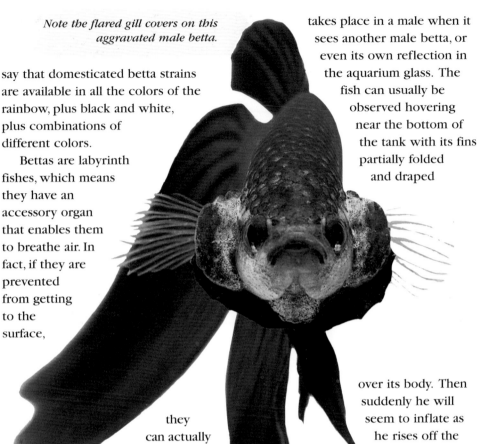

say that domesticated betta strains are available in all the colors of the rainbow, plus black and white, plus combinations of different colors.

Bettas are labyrinth fishes, which means they have an accessory organ that enables them to breathe air. In fact, if they are prevented from getting to the surface, they can actually "drown," since they will not get sufficient oxygen from the water and of course die. This evolutionary adaptation serves them very well in the often oxygen-poor stagnant swamps in which they live, but due to this they must always have direct access to the water's surface.

Betta Magic

One of the most fascinating aspects bettas exhibit is the transformation that takes place in a male when it sees another male betta, or even its own reflection in the aquarium glass. The fish can usually be observed hovering near the bottom of the tank with its fins partially folded and draped over its body. Then suddenly he will seem to inflate as he rises off the bottom, unfurls his fins, and spreads them to the extreme. His already bright colors may brighten even more, and he flares his gill covers out, making his face appear many times larger than normal. He lunges at the intruder (or reflection) and also presents his side, flaring his fins and shuddering his body. A male that is ready to breed will perform a very similar display when he sees a female.

Bettas

Another seemingly magical aspect of bettas is the variety and shapes and colors they come in. It is almost as if breeders can fill in a blank betta outline with any colors they want! Many people find it impossible to select one favorite-colored betta, and they wind up purchasing several of

Air Breathing

Bettas have gills and obtain oxygen from water like other fish, but they also have a labyrinth organ through which they obtain oxygen from the air. They are unable to get sufficient oxygen through their gills, so they must have access to air.

different colors. We will discuss betta colors and fin types in Chapter 6.

Relaxation & Fascination

Watching any aquarium is relaxing and can even be therapeutic. Unfortunately, watching many a single betta in bowls is downright boring. Slowed down by overly cold water, cramped in a tiny space, starved for protein, and injured by ammonia burn, many male bettas simply deplete all their energy just to exist, so they hardly move and don't seem able to pay attention to their surroundings.

Properly cared for, bettas are as interesting as any other tropical fish, and they will greet you eagerly at the front glass, dancing in anticipation of some food. They will also prowl their space, alert for food or foe. These fish are slow and deliberate, not bustling, but they are lively when maintained under the right conditions.

Betta Bowl Bunk

A pathetic betta languishing in a typical betta bowl or betta vase does not at all act normally of course. Although it is quite possible to keep a betta properly in a small vessel such as a bowl or a vase, this type of maintenance requires special attention and we will treat this topic in more detail in the following chapters. In this introduction, we will simply debunk several common beliefs about maintaining bettas to help you decide if a betta really is the right fish choice for you.

Bunk: No Size is Too Small

Bettas need some exercise; they have to have room to actually swim. Thus, bigger is better and containers for bettas should be at least 6 inches (15 cm) across.

Bunk: Volume is Unimportant

The ability to breathe air greatly minimizes a betta's need for sufficient water to obtain its oxygen needs, but it has no affect whatsoever on the fish's need for sufficient water into which its wastes can dissolve. The total volume of the water influences maintenance regimes: If you only want to change your betta's water once a week, you should give your fish at least a gallon (4 liters) of water. A quart or liter of water will last a single betta only two or three days, at which time the water will become toxically laden with wastes. In similar ratios, a half quart or half liter will only last a day or two, and a betta in a bowl that holds a mere cup (250 ml) of water will need a complete water change at least once a day. A good filtration system will stretch these times out considerably, however.

Bettas should have the ability to get some exercise. Jars like this are fine for showing or transporting but not usually for housing.

Bettas are tropical fish, and therefore need tropical temperatures to remain healthy.

Bunk: Room Temperature is Fine

While a betta will survive at room temperature, it will not thrive. Bettas need warmth, as they are tropical fish from very warm habitats. The best water temperature for them is about 80°F (27°C). To maintain this temperature, an aquarium heater is almost always necessary.

Bunk: Bettas Eat Plant Roots

Bettas are meat eaters and cannot live off plant roots. In the wild they may nibble on some algae, but their main diet is worms, insects, and small crustaceans. They must be fed, and they must be fed meat-based foods.

Are you Still Interested?

If you would still like to acquire a betta, great! It is important to point out a few possible negatives involved in betta keeping, so that you can make a fully informed decision.

Life Span

Compared to other fish genera, bettas are not particularly long lived. Even within this parameter, many die premature deaths due to general misinformation about maintaining betta bowls. Since you will know how to properly care for your betta after reading this book, premature death will not be an issue, but you are still looking at a one- to three-year typical life span for bettas.

One reason for a short life span in your tank is that people prefer buying already a year or more of age when you get it.

Also, bowl life, like couch potato life for humans, increases the chance of early death from obesity and degenerative diseases. In fact, some people who have kept some very old bettas (nine years or more) attribute their fish's longevity to their practice of gently chasing their bettas around the tank every day, which provides their bettas with the type of exercise they would get if they had to look for food and escape predators in the wild.

a male betta that has full fin growth. Bettas reach sexual maturity before they are fully developed, so it is common for dealers to sell ex-breeders. This way betta breeders get several spawns to justify the expense of keeping the fish until they have full finnage, and betta lovers get the long fins they want, but it also means that any fish you may purchase with resplendent fins is

Healthy bettas can live for several years if cared for properly.

This would suggest that bettas kept in regular community aquariums will be healthier and live longer than bettas

Fascinating Fins

Children (of all ages!) are fascinated by the showy display of a male betta. With supervision, your child can place a small mirror next to the betta tank and watch him strut his stuff. This is good exercise for the fish, and it makes a great show.

in bowls, but I don't know of any data to either support or disclaim this theory.

The most significant factors regarding betta life span, however, derive from the natural environment in which bettas have evolved. Particular circumstances in the wild favor adaptations like early breeding rather than those that produce long life. A delayed rainy season, a dry rice paddy after it drains, or similar events can kill off bettas in the wild, and predators

abound. Although they are not annual fish, bettas are found in some very seasonal habitats. Even bettas that do not live to see the next rainy season are able to leave descendants, and some of these scatter to new habitats before it is too late. Like most fish in such environments, bettas grow quickly, spawn when young, and produce many offspring. They do not, however, live many years. Although there are exceptions, most bettas will die somewhere within the first four years.

Fighting Behavior

Male bettas are naturally belligerent toward each other. You've already seen that a male betta will make a vivid display when facing another of his species, whether male or female. In either case, all this posturing is soon followed by an attack if the new fish does not retreat. Another male will probably respond with a flaring

Desktop Betta Bowls

Betta bowls can be a nice display, but they must be set up with the needs of the fish in mind. As beautiful as they are, bettas are living creatures that must be properly cared for, not just ornaments.

Hobbyists should never house multiple male bettas in one tank!

display of his own, and this quickly leads to actual combat, with fins and scales being damaged. If the newcomer is a receptive female, the courtship will soon progress to luring the female under the male's nest, but if she is not ready to lay eggs, she, too, will be attacked.

For this reason it is very important never to keep a male betta with any other bettas, unless you are trying to breed them. Although occasionally female bettas will also fight, they usually get along well together, but males will never coexist peacefully. So, you can keep a male betta by himself, or with appropriate non-betta tank-mates, but only females can ever be kept together.

Chapter 2

Getting Started and Keeping it

Running

There are two ways to keep a male betta: by himself or in a community of peaceful fishes in a larger aquarium. In the latter case, the betta is simply another tank inhabitant, and the major consideration is that there are no nippy tankmates that will shred his fins or otherwise harass him. We will therefore focus here on keeping a single male betta as a display.

Betta Bowl Selection & Set Up

Despite their popularity, many "betta bowl" setups are horribly inadequate for the fish. This bad situation is even more unfortunate because it is not difficult to provide a proper environment for a betta. Problems arise due to the fact that the air-breathing ability of these fish makes it possible to keep them in very small volumes of water, but keeping fish in small volumes of water is fraught with difficulties. In addition, several falsehoods are frequently circulated about betta bowls, and these lead to further mistreatment of the fish. We touched on these in the last chapter, but now we can look at them in more detail.

Bowl Size

A puppy will not suffocate in a wire-mesh crate so small it can barely turn around, but that does not mean such a

Keep it Covered

Bettas are very good jumpers. It is almost inevitable that they will jump out of an uncovered container.

setup is sufficient for the animal. Just because a betta will not suffocate in a bowl of water so small that it can barely turn around also does not mean such a setup is sufficient for the animal.

On the other hand, bettas are not terribly active fish. They do not school. They do not chase prey through open water. In the wild, a male betta defends a rather small territory around its nest, which is usually centered on a clump of grass or other vegetation. They are ambush predators, normally lurking

Myth & Reality

The ability of a betta to breathe air to supplement oxygen dissolved in the water leads some people to the conclusion that a betta doesn't need very much water. Many people claim that a betta will thrive in a vase set on a desk among the roots of a plant, feeding on the roots and having the plant use up all its wastes. They say it doesn't need any additional heat, filtration, feeding, or water changes. This is completely untrue.

Yes, a betta can be maintained in a bowl, with or without a plant, but no, it will not eat plant roots, and it does need water changes, and probably heating, too.

Contrary to popular belief,
bettas do not eat plant roots!

among vegetation, always attentive to any small invertebrate that crawls or swims into view. In addition, male bettas of fancy strains typically have extremely long fins that make rapid swimming impossible. Thus, they do not need large amounts of open water for swimming; they do, however, need some room for exercise. A bowl large enough for the fish to swim several body lengths in every direction is adequate, and this is still a rather small container, suitable for a desktop display.

Bowl Placement

Many people want a betta bowl as an ornamental display on a desk or table. As long as the bowl will not receive direct sunlight, this is fine. Although direct sun is not recommended for any aquarium, a small betta bowl will very quickly overheat in bright sun. Even if the water in the bowl does not get hot enough to kill the betta outright, any extreme and rapid changes in water temperature will stress the fish and weaken its immune system.

You should, of course, also avoid locations near outside doors that might permit the bowl to become chilled regularly, or in places where the bowl will be subjected to frequent jarring, such as on top of a busy file cabinet. The top of appliances like televisions not only exposes the bowl to possible overheating, it also threatens the electronics with water spillage.

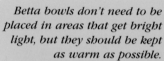

Betta bowls don't need to be placed in areas that get bright light, but they should be kept as warm as possible.

Filtration & Aeration

Technically, aeration is not an important consideration for a betta bowl, since the fish can get the oxygen it needs from breathing air. Filtration, on the other hand, is an important consideration. The idea of keeping a single betta in a jar or bowl is borrowed from betta breeders, who maintain hundreds of jars for growing out the males from their spawns.

Remember that bettas breathe from the surface, so any cover on the bowl should not be in direct contact with the water. An air pocket is essential.

Unfortunately, the painstaking care regimen of the betta breeder was not borrowed along with the bowl idea. Very frequent water changes are used by breeders to keep their jarred bettas healthy—two or more complete changes per week for quart jars, more often for smaller volumes. In recent years this has been replaced in many cases with systems which employ central filtration for betta vessels. Various flow-through setups provide each jar or section with a constant supply of clean, filtered water. In effect, each betta obtains the benefits of living in many gallons of filtered water even though he is confined to a small space and kept separate from all the other fish in the system.

It is actually very rare to see a betta in an unfiltered bowl that does not suffer from visible ammonia burn on its fins. When a fish reaches this state, it is certain that it will have suffered severe ammonia damage to its delicate gill tissues as well. Although most people think of filtration in terms of keeping the bowl clean and the water clear, the most crucial aspect of filtration is biofiltration—the use of bacterial colonies to process ammonia and nitrite in the water. These two toxic wastes are invisible, however, and they can injure or kill a fish long before the bowl becomes visibly dirty.

The most common method commercial breeders use is easily adapted to a single betta bowl setup. They have two sets of jars: one houses bettas, while the other is ready with conditioned water of the proper temperature. To change the water, a jar is dumped into a net, the fish is placed into a clean jar, and the original jar is cleaned, refilled, and set aside for the next round of water changes.

With sufficient water changes—such as a complete water change daily—a small betta bowl can get by without other filtration. There are, however, mini filters available that can operate on a betta display, making it possible to change the water only once or twice a week. A small air-operated sponge filter is perfect for a betta container, and it provides one of the best biofilters.

Lighting & Temperature Control

We've already discussed the danger of direct sunlight on a betta bowl, but artificial lighting is certainly possible, and some bettas positively glow under the correct type of light. Overheating is again a concern with many light fixtures, but ones designed for betta bowls are typically raised above the bowl, providing plenty of airspace to insulate the water from the heat produced by the lamp. Regular room light, however, is fine from the fish's point of view, and if you are happy with it, you do not need any supplemental light for the bowl. Temperature control is still a

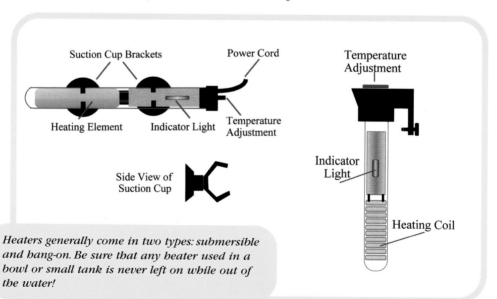

Side View of Suction Cup

Heaters generally come in two types: submersible and hang-on. Be sure that any heater used in a bowl or small tank is never left on while out of the water!

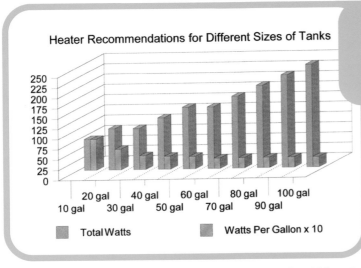

Heater Recommendations for Different Sizes of Tanks

250
225
200
175
150
125
100
75
50
25
0

10 gal 20 gal 30 gal 40 gal 50 gal 60 gal 70 gal 80 gal 90 gal 100 gal

■ Total Watts   ■ Watts Per Gallon x 10

This illustration shows the recommended heaters for different aquariums.

commonly very warm. The ideal temperature range for bettas is about 76° to 84°F (25° to 29°C), with the warmer end of the range best for breeding.

problem, no matter how little lighting you use. This is because bettas are tropical fish. Moreover, they are found naturally in very shallow swamps and rice paddies, where the water is

It should be obvious from these figures that typical room temperatures, at least during the winter, are insufficient for the proper maintenance of bettas. Normal room temperatures will not usually kill bettas directly, but consistently cool water will weaken the fish.

Substrates come in a wide assortment of colors and grains. Use whichever is most appealing to you, as the bettas don't seem to mind either way,

Bettas tend to show their colors off a little nicer when kept in nicely aquascaped bowls or tanks.

Also, much of the lethargy observed in jarred bettas can be attributed to low temperatures. If you observe a male betta kept in a 5-gallon (19-liter) bowl with a heater and

Small pieces of rainbow rock are commonly used in bettas bowls and small aquariums.

filtration, you will see how this fish naturally acts. It is simply not normal for them to lie on the bottom of the bowl all day, rising only to gulp air or grab some food.

The problem with heaters and betta bowls is that a small quantity of water heats up and cools off too rapidly. Even a very small heater will alternately cook and chill the fish. Because of the popularity of betta bowls, very low-wattage heaters have become available, but they still need a decent volume of water to be effective and safe. Temperature is something you can understand and directly perceive, but even more important is the buildup of wastes in small volumes of water. If a bowl is too small to heat properly, it is also probably too small to maintain a betta due to waste accumulation.

Substrate & Decorations

A popular substrate in many betta bowls is smooth round pebbles. This is an unsafe choice, since uneaten food

and fish wastes will disappear down the large spaces between the stones. There they decompose, adding to the ammonia bioload. Occasionally a betta will get caught by its head when it tries to poke down into the pebbles for a morsel of food; this can result in injury or death. If you want a substrate, use fine gravel. In a small container, gravel is a problem, however. Not only will it trap debris, including uneaten food, it will make water changing problematic. You must make sure that the gravel is completely cleaned with each water change.

A betta bowl is typically space challenged already, so adding ornaments will only take up valuable space. If you want decorations, make sure the bowl is large enough to provide space for the fish even after the ornaments are added.

Plants

Plants are welcome in a betta bowl. These can be terrestrial plants with

their roots in the water (provided the plant does not prevent the fish from reaching the surface to breathe air), but fully aquatic plants are also fine. Plants will take up some fish wastes, and they provide a natural refuge for the fish. The biofiltration capability of bacteria on plant leaves and roots is usually negligible in an aquarium, but in a small betta bowl the contribution can be significant. Plant species that have low light requirements such as Java moss and Java fern are very popular among betta keepers. Of course, plants whose roots are in a betta bowl should also require low light as well, since placing the bowl in a sunny window is not an option.

Cycling

You hear a lot about "cycling" an aquarium, but this concept is not often brought up with regard to betta bowls. The reason is quite simple: The notion of cycling an aquarium is actually a matter of establishing a biofilter, and few betta bowls have any biofilter at all. Not all aquariums have biofilters; many

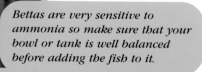

Bettas are very sensitive to ammonia so make sure that your bowl or tank is well balanced before adding the fish to it.

Testing your water's quality should be done on a weekly basis at least.

discus breeders use completely bare tanks, but they change all of the water once or twice daily. This way, fish wastes—especially the highly toxic ammonia—never accumulate. When a bacterial biofilter is unavailable, frequent water changes are the only way to keep ammonia from accumulating.

The process called "cycling" requires a period up to six weeks long in which ammonia is allowed to build up, fueling the growth of one type of bacteria in the filter medium (often a foam sponge). These bacteria convert the ammonia to nitrite—another toxic waste. As nitrite builds up, a second type of bacteria colonizes the filter; these convert nitrite to nitrate, which is harmful only in high concentrations. Trying to cycle a filter in a tiny betta bowl will severely stress the poor fish, since ammonia (and later nitrite) will accumulate to extreme levels before the bacterial colonies have time to become established. Therefore, the

best way to cycle a betta bowl filter is to run it for several weeks on a well-stocked aquarium. Then, when the filter is mature, you can move it to the betta bowl and introduce the betta at the same time.

Testing, Testing...123

It is easy to monitor ammonia and nitrite levels, which should remain at zero levels at all times in the fish's water. Test kits that typically give results categorized within ranges of safe, concern, and danger are available. If you ever get measurable levels of ammonia or nitrite in your betta's water, perform a water change immediately to correct the situation, and step up your changing regimen so it doesn't happen again.

SMALL FRY

The Basic Elements for Success

Children need to understand that keeping a live animal requires certain "life support." Explain how the heater and filter make the conditions optimal for a pet betta.

Chapter 3

Eating Well

Feeding bettas, like feeding any pet, is basic to proper husbandry. With the right diet, your betta will thrive. Bettas are naturally carnivorous; their diet consists almost entirely of tiny invertebrates such as insects, worms, and crustaceans. When otherwise-starved, bettas are observed pecking on plant roots; they are actually picking off various microorganisms living on the roots.

Although bettas will benefit from a little vegetation (normally algae) in their diet, they should have primarily meat-based foods. A major factor to consider is that a single betta does not need very much food at all, and a small volume of water is easily polluted by overfeeding. In addition, bettas have small mouths, designed for eating very small creatures, so they need their food provided in suitably sized pieces.

Bettas are mostly surface feeders, and their food should be of the floating type.

Besides proteins, bettas need general dietary components such as carbohydrates, fats, roughage, and vitamins and minerals. Unlike the mammals with which you might be familiar, fish are among those animals that often derive their coloration from pigments ingested with their food. Red and yellow pigmentation is especially reliant on carotenoids from food. Thus, proper feeding can enhance the colors of your fish.

Basic Betta Nutrition

As predators, bettas require a high-protein diet. Like any fish, they will eat another fish small enough to swallow, but they do not generally hunt down, kill, and tear apart their prey. Instead they are micropredators, mainly eating animals small enough to swallow whole or in a couple of bites. They will grab a larger worm and rip a piece off to swallow, but they usually target one-bite meals.

Female bettas, like this one, need the proper nutrition in order to produce healthy, viable eggs.

Little is known, however, about the specific dietary needs of most tropical fishes. This is because research on this topic is rarely funded; instead, projects investigate the needs of aquacultured fishes—those raised for human consumption. The best way to make up for the lack of specific knowledge is to feed a varied diet. Alternating among several foods makes it much more likely that your betta's diet will contain everything it needs; a substance lacking in one food will probably be in another one, and vice versa.

Fortunately, through testing, trials, and experience, many manufacturers have produced formulae that promote natural health, growth, and coloration in tropical fishes. These make an excellent foundation for your betta's diet.

Commercial Foods

Feeding bettas is easier today than ever, as many manufacturers produce foods perfect for these fish. These come in various forms.

Dry Foods

Dry foods are available in three basic types: flakes, pellets/sticks, and wafers. When the formula is rolled into very thin sheets and dried, the result is flakes of various sizes. You can easily crush the flakes between your fingers to produce smaller flakes or even pulverized, or powdered, food. Pellets and sticks are produced when the formulation is extruded rather than rolled thin. There are many pellets on the market that will provide a good basic diet for your betta. Some are specially formulated for bettas and packed in a handy dispenser package that permits you to tap out single pellets—very useful when feeding just one fish. Only very small pellets are suitable for bettas,

Small floating pellets are one of the best, and easiest-to-use, types of foods available for bettas.

since they have rather small mouths.

Wafers are disks of food, and they are designed for bottom feeders like loaches and catfish. A hungry betta will certainly pick at a wafer, but even the smallest wafer is way too much food for a betta, and bettas usually prefer to pick their food from the surface anyway.

Frozen Foods

Many frozen foods are excellent for a betta, including brine shrimp and bloodworms. The major drawback to these foods for a betta in a bowl is that it is very difficult to feed only a few frozen organisms, and putting in too big a morsel of frozen food will quickly foul the water. In tanks with other fish, bettas will gladly join the feeding frenzy when

Small shrimps are available in freeze-dried form and make a great addition to the diet of all bettas.

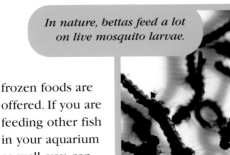

In nature, bettas feed a lot on live mosquito larvae.

frozen foods are offered. If you are feeding other fish in your aquarium as well, you can let a small piece defrost in a bit of water, then siphon out just a few worms or shrimp to give to your betta and give the rest to the other fish. Obviously frozen foods must be kept frozen. Never feed foods that have thawed and refrozen, as they may kill your fish. To use, just break off an appropriate sized piece and drop it into the tank.

Freeze-Dried Foods

Freeze drying produces foods that have almost the same appeal to fish as the frozen variety, but they are much more convenient. For example, you can pick up just one or two freeze-dried blood-worms to give to your betta.

Freeze-dried foods should be kept in an airtight container, but they do not need refrigeration. The fine particles left at the bottom of the package make ideal food for fry.

Better Than Fresh

Often frozen or freeze dried foods are higher in nutrition than live foods. This is because they are processed very soon after harvesting, whereas living organisms are shipped and stored for a considerable amount of time. During this time they are often not fed, and aquatic animals may be kept in increasingly foul water. Do not assume that a lively, wriggling food item is nutritionally superior to the processed frozen or freeze-dried forms.

Live Foods

Bettas love live foods, and while they can live long, healthy lives on only prepared foods, they will enjoy live foods as a treat. Brine shrimp, black-worms, and bloodworms are often available at local retailers, and mosquito larvae and daphnia are easily collected. Microworms (washed clean of any culture medium), white worms, Grindal worms, and wingless fruit flies can be cultured to provide a steady supply of live foods for your betta. As with prepared foods, you must be very careful not to overfeed live foods. Several live foods, however, will remain alive for quite some time in the water, enabling your fish to feed over extended periods without the danger of decomposition.

How Much to Feed?

We've already mentioned the dangers of overfeeding, which are greatly compounded when one fish is being kept in a small volume of water. In many cases, a single morsel (pellet, live organism, or flake) is sufficient as a

Bettas are active hunters when they have to be but they prefer to let the food come to them.

Live tubifex worms are often used to feed bettas, but they can cause health issues due to where they are collected from so be cautious and use sparingly.

meal for a betta. Keep in mind that fish are cold blooded. This is significant when talking about nutrition, since a fish does not use food to produce body heat. Much of the food eaten by a warm-blooded animal is metabolized just to maintain the proper body temperature, but cold-blooded animals, which do not maintain a set temperature, have much lower caloric requirements. Many mammals will starve to death in a few days without food; fish, on the other hand, can fast

for a week or two without suffering injury. Both the frequency and the amount of food required by a fish or a reptile is considerably less than for a similarly sized mammal.

In addition, since a betta typically waits for food to come to him, he is adapted to feast when food is available and to wait out the lean times. In captivity, the fish is inclined to overeat to the point of illness. Constant overeating without fasting periods leads to obesity and degenerative diseases, but even more serious health problems can arise from single instances of gross overeating. A betta will stuff itself until its belly is a huge bulge with scales distended. This is never good, and it can be fatal if impaction occurs.

Bettas Love Bugs!

Insects are natural food for a betta. Not all bugs, however, are suitable for your pet. Probably the best insect to feed your fish is the wingless fruit fly, which you can culture easily in small bottles.

Don't Be a Pushover

Feed with your brain, not with your heart. Give your betta the right amount of food, and do not give in to his protests of starvation, which he will continue long after he has had enough to eat.

The best regimen for betta meals is to feed several extremely small meals per day, occasionally skipping a meal or two, and once in a while skipping a day completely. What is an extremely small meal for a betta? One pellet. One fruit fly. One or two bloodworms. This will approximate the way a wild betta eats, catching a bug or a worm every once in a while, but never finding a plethora of food.

Feeding Problems

Besides overfeeding, problems can arise either with the food or with the fish itself.

Improper Diet

As already explained, feeding a variety of foods is the best way to ensure proper nutrition, especially if the foundation of the diet is a formulation designed specifically for bettas. Southeast Asian betta breeders often feed live foods exclusively with superb results, but few Western breeders do the same. In Asia, a great variety of live foods is readily available and inexpensive—and fish stores everywhere stock several types of mosquito and other insect larvae, worms, and even tiny baby fish as food.

In the Americas and Europe, most live foods must be cultured at home, since they are available in very limited quantities at pet shops. The ready availability of excellent prepared foods at much lower prices than live foods makes it much easier for Western betta keepers to use the commercial foods.

Loss of Appetite

A betta should always be hungry, even after he is fed. If he lies, belly extended, at the bottom of his bowl, apathetic to the food you add, then you have certainly overfed him. But what if he doesn't take food, even when he hasn't been recently fed?

Loss of appetite is almost always a very bad sign, as it indicates an unhealthy fish. The only exception is a betta that is spawning, or tending a nest. Many refuse to be distracted by food, which should never be offered to an actively spawning pair. It is generally not necessary to feed a male with eggs in his nest, though you may if he seems

Varying the diet of bettas is important in preventing your fish from becoming used to only one type of food.

willing to leave his brood for a moment to eat.

In all other cases, a betta refusing food should, before anything else, be given a water change. Deteriorating water conditions will often kill a betta's appetite, and fresh water will quickly restore it. If he still isn't hungry a while after the water change, examine him closely for signs of disease, and treat him accordingly. Most of the time, however, keeping his water clean will do the trick.

Spoiling

An occasional problem is spoiling. No, we're not talking about the spoilage of food (which you of course would guard against), but spoiling your fish. It is very easy for fish to train their keepers, not only to feed them too often, but even to provide a single favored food. A betta can learn that if he refuses one food, you will provide another one. This can lead to dietary deficiencies. Vary the diet to keep your fish guessing, and you will be providing balanced fare for him.

SMALL FRY

Lock Up the Food

If you have small children in the house, you should handle your betta's food the same as you would a medication, keeping it out of reach of little hands at all times. You can certainly enlist a child's help in feeding your betta, but the child must understand that you determine the amount and frequency of the feedings. A child's generosity will indubitably lead to your betta's death if the youngster gains access to the food container and dumps it into the betta bowl.

Eating Well

Chapter 4

Feeling Good

A healthy betta has good color, perfect fins that he extends fully, an interest in what is going on outside his bowl, a good appetite, and often a bubblenest. A sick betta may not show any of these variables, and when several are missing, things are getting serious.

ortunately, maintaining a betta in good health is not difficult. We've already seen how proper space, temperature, and water conditions eliminate the lackluster appearance and lethargy of many unfortunate desktop bettas, but what about when a properly cared-for betta falls ill?

Injuries

A betta can be injured by other fish, by netting, or by sharp edges of substrate or ornaments. Such injuries include bruises, cuts, missing scales, and ripped fins. In most cases these will heal on their own. Be especially careful to maintain water cleanliness to minimize the chance of infection, but otherwise just keep an eye on the fish. Fortunately, fish usually heal quickly, and they are able to regenerate lost pieces of their fins completely.

Diseases

Fish ailments are frequently misdiagnosed, and pet fish are often treated with the wrong medications or overmedicated. Since the proper diagnosis and treatment of many diseases requires clinical tests and professional care by a veterinarian, the cost of such medical therapy is many times the value of a small fish, and typically only people with extremely valuable fish—like an expensive koi—take this route. Fortunately, bettas don't usually

Bettas are prone to fin injuries.

Clamped fins are telltale sign of a problem.

If not removed from the water, those cysts will ripen and release hundreds of new parasites that will reinfest the fish.

You can buy medications that will eliminate the infection, but you must be extremely careful as to correct dosage amounts when dealing with very small volumes of water. Most breeders prefer the heat and salt treatment.

contract any of those diseases, and the vast majority of bouts with illness will involve one of two major culprits.

Ich

The ich protozoan (short for *Ichthyophthirius* and pronounced "ick") produces white spots on a fish; these are formed by parasites embedded in the fish's skin. They also attack the gills, where they are much more difficult to detect—and much more dangerous. This is a common disease that is easily taken care of, but if it goes untreated, it is usually fatal. A betta with ich can be successfully treated by raising the water temperature to 90°F (32°C) and adding a bit of salt to the water. Change the water completely at least once, preferably twice, a day; this removes the free-swimming stage of the parasite, as well as the cysts which fall off the fish.

SMALL FRY

Teaching Respect for Living Beings

A pet betta can teach a youngster how to respect other living beings. By involving the child in the regular care of the fish, you can demonstrate the proper treatment of animals, with a concern for their well-being.

Velvet

Velvet is the other protozoan disease that you are likely to come across. These parasites show up as copper yellow spots on the fish. If ich makes a fish look salted, velvet makes it look sanded. You may need to shine a flashlight on the fish to see the spots, which are smaller and less visible than ich cysts.

This disease is most common in juvenile bettas and is often associated with deteriorating water conditions. It can be such a problem with betta fry that many breeders use salt in the water at all times as a preventative. Unfortunately, few agree on the appropriate dose; recommendations range from a tablespoon per gallon to a teaspoon per five gallons—a fifteen-

Salt

Aquarium salt is one of the oldest, and still one of the best, treatments for a variety of fish ailments.

Many betta breeders use salt as a prophylactic, keeping small concentrations in the water of their breeding tanks at all times.

fold difference! It is a good thing bettas have fairly good salt tolerance. As with ich, there are commercial medications that will deal with the infection, though salt is also effective.

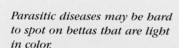

Parasitic diseases may be hard to spot on bettas that are light in color.

Bettas that have had their fins damaged are highly prone to fin rot.

Daily water changes are also indicated, both to remove free-swimming parasites and to keep dissolved wastes from accumulating.

Fin Rot

Keeping bettas in filthy water leads first to fin burn, then to fin rot as infections take hold on the damaged tissue. Putting—and keeping—the affected fish in clean water is the major treatment. Remember that once the fins are burned, so are the gills. Long after another fish would have died from gill burn, a betta will still be alive due to its ability to breathe air, which is why so many unfortunate bettas wind up in filthy little bowls.

If clean water is insufficient, you will have to use commercial medications to eliminate the fin rot infection. Once the damage is halted, the fish can regenerate its fins, though they will probably not be as grand as they were originally, and they may not have normal coloration. Healing fin

Newly acquired bettas should always be quarantined for at least 2 weeks before placing them in a show tank or other, more permanent home.

rot is much more difficult for the fish than when a fin is just ripped or cut off; in that case, healing is usually complete.

Quarantine & Prevention

It may surprise you to hear that many long-time betta fanciers have almost no experience with disease. That is because they quarantine any new fish they obtain and practice disease prevention. There are only two ways your fish can come down with an illness from a pathogen: either a new

Watch the Drugs!

Remember that aquarium medications are for treating a properly diagnosed illness. If a fish looks sick and you just dump in one—or worse, several—medications, you are more likely to harm rather than help your fish. The very best pick-me-up tonic for your betta is a complete water change.

not have to come into contact to spread disease; nets, hands, and hoses can transfer pathogens from one container to another.

Prevention

All of the topics of this book until now have been concerned with the proper care of bettas, and that is exactly what disease prevention is: proper care. This consists of clean water, proper temperature, and good food in appropriate amounts. Following that regimen will go so far in keeping your betta healthy that it is quite possible you will never experience any health problems with your pet.

The converse is also true: dirty water, chilly temperatures, and inadequate feeding (or overfeeding) will quickly bring the healthiest betta down to illness and misery.

45

Feeling Good

fish introduces the pathogen to your tank and infects your other fish, or a pathogen against which your fish have resistance gets the upper hand because your fish become stressed, and their immune response fails.

Quarantine

Any fish (betta or not) should be kept by itself, with no shared water source, for a month after you bring it home. During that time any disease it is carrying will probably manifest itself, and you can treat the fish to eliminate the infection. It is important to remember that fish do

Water Changes

When changing your betta's water, use water of the same temperature and which has also been treated to remove any chlorine compounds your municipal water supply uses as sanitizers. This prevents shocking or poisoning your fish.

Chapter 5

Getting Along

Bettas are definitely not social animals. There are three conditions in which they will have to interact with other fish: living in community tanks, living separately but side-by-side with other males, and being involved in breeding situations. Unless you are keeping a single betta by himself, you should take several factors into account when housing your fish.

Community Tanks

Bettas are underutilized as community fish. I have even heard people express surprise that they don't have to be kept alone in a bowl. At the same time, I often see bettas in community aquariums that would definitely prefer being kept alone, as their fins are often torn and ragged. So, if you want to add the beauty and grace of a male betta to a community, make sure that it's not going to become mutilated by his tankmates.

Tankmates

Bettas are very much live-and-let-live fish when it comes to other species. Provided a fish is too large for a betta to swallow, and provided it's not another betta, the betta will usually ignore it. On the other hand, with its bright colors and long, flowing fins, a

male betta is a likely target for any fin nippers. In addition, its relatively sedentary life style and deliberate movements will invite pestering by inquisitive or boisterous tankmates, as well as attack from any territorial fish that do not want him hanging around. Last, aggressive feeders will get all the food before the betta gets a chance. Thus, betta tankmates should be calm, peaceful, nonaggressive, nonterritorial species.

48

Bettas

Cory cats make good tankmates for bettas.

Bettas are generally loners and don't need the company of other fishes— especially other bettas!

White clouds are peaceful and can be placed in an aquarium with a betta.

Most livebearers, some small tetras, *Corydoras* catfish, white clouds, and rasboras are among the good choices. Most barbs are too nippy, but in a large tank a school of one of the more peaceful species, like the cherry barb (*Puntius titteya*), may work well. Although barbs should never be kept alone or in pairs, it is especially important to maintain them in schools of six or more when there is a betta in the tank—the fish are kept busy interacting with each other, and they generally stay out of the betta's business.

Setup

A healthy betta in a heated and filtered

SMALL FRY

Explaining Fish Compatibility

It's natural that a child will want to keep more than one betta, or to give a betta in a bowl some other fish for company. Explain that bettas are grumpy with each other and will fight, and that most other species of fish cannot be kept in a bowl because they don't breathe air the way the betta can.

Bettas will need a few days to adjust to their new setup.

aquarium is much more active than one kept in a tiny unfiltered bowl at room temperature, but it is still lethargic compared to most typical community species. Also, its long fins make it difficult for the betta to swim very vigorously; thus, it does not do well with powerful currents or substantial water depths.

Bettas are not native to fast-flowing waters, so even short-finned varieties are not equipped to handle strong currents. The filter in a betta tank should produce very little current. Bubble-up filters are great, as are power filters that

Kin Make Bad Choices

Besides fin nippers, hyperactive, and aggressive fishes, it is best to avoid closely related species like gouramis. Bettas and gouramis are similar enough that they usually see each other as direct competitors and are likely to try to chase each other off.

return the water in a cascade or spray bar rather than in a stream or a concentrated jet. Powerheads should not be used in a tank housing a betta.

In the wild, bettas can often be found in an inch or two (2 to 5 cm) of water. They typically lurk among some vegetation, rising to the surface to catch an insect, repair a bubblenest, or gulp some air. They try to live the same way in an aquarium. If the aquarium is too deep, they seem to struggle when making their trips to the surface. Aquariums less than a foot (30 cm) deep are best, therefore. This does not restrict you

Social Issues

You might wonder how bettas live in the wild, if they cannot be kept with each other. The answer is simple: When two bettas fight, one will eventually be overpowered. At this point, the loser takes off, making tracks quickly into the undergrowth. The victor gloats in his territory. In a small aquarium, the loser cannot escape, and his opponent continues to beat on him, confused as to why he won't just leave.

to small communities, since there are many stock tank sizes in this category, including the impressive 4-foot (122-cm) long, 33-gallon (125-liter) tank. Such long, low tanks are best for a community that includes bettas. Floating plants, however, enable a betta to inhabit the surface of even very deep aquariums and still feel secure. Bettas love to rest among vegetation, and floating vegetation (living or plastic) gives them a perch near the surface, where they like to be.

Betta Communities
The well-known pugnacious nature of the betta makes it hard for many people to believe that this fish can be kept in communities, and, though possible, it is rarely done. We will discuss the mechanics of such communities as breeding setups more fully in Chapter 7, but let's look at the environmental basis of bettas in the wild for them.

Natural Sites
In the wild, bettas inhabit standing water in swamps, rice paddies, and flooded areas. The water is usually extremely shallow. This affords obvious protection from predation by large fish, since only the smallest fish can navigate the vegetation-choked, shallow water. The use of a nest of bubbles, into which the eggs are placed, keeps the eggs out of the oxygen-deprived

Regardless of how beautiful the betta is, and how nice it would look in a community tank, it is always best to keep them alone.

*Bettas should be provided with some
form of natural cover in their tank.*

water, and keeps them moist while surrounded by oxygen-laden air. (After all, the eggs can't swim to the surface for a periodic breath of air.)

The males stake out a small territory around their nest site, which might be a floating leaf or a clump of grass sticking out of the water. He drives away any fish that comes into this area, unless it is a female ready to spawn, in which case he courts and spawns with her.

Females do not maintain territories, but when they are full of eggs, they enter a male's territory for spawning.

Sometimes this involves a bit of dexterity, since males have been known to set up their nests in water that oozes into a water buffalo's hoofprint! The female fish has to get to such a site by slithering and flopping across the swamp.

Out of Sight, Out of Mind

Thus, an Asian swamp might house a number of male bettas, each tending a nest in an isolated territory. This isolation can be actual—as in a flooded hoofprint—or functional, such as separation by a tangle of aquatic vegetation or a grassy hummock that blocks the line of sight between nests. Thus, the keys to a betta community are adequate space for numerous territories and sufficient vegetation.

Side-By-Side Males

Many people maintain a row of bettas, either in jars lined up or in a single vessel fitted with partitions. Besides providing a display of many different males, perhaps each of a different color, this permits viewing the elaborate displays the fish make as they try to drive each other away—and therein lies the controversy.

The vehemence with which a male betta will attempt to get at his neighbor through the walls of the vessels is amazing, and it is easy for a human watching the display to project a great deal of frustration onto the fish's psyche. This leads to questions of cruelty: isn't it mean to make the fish struggle like that, driven by instinct to fight a battle it can never win? What people often fail to take into

Bettas are extremely territorial when it comes to other bettas—especially other males!

account is the ethological notion of habituation. Whether it is caution toward a new object in the environment, aggression toward a territorial intruder, sexual response to a potential mate, or even fear of a predator, an animal's response to an incessant stimulus is habituation—the instinctive response attenuates until it ceases altogether. In the betta's case, the males soon habituate to each other's presence and stop displaying. In fact, they often settle down to building nests, just as they would in the wild after chasing off an intruding male.

In fact, this is precisely why retailers often keep cards between their jars of male bettas. When a customer is interested, they want to be able to pull out a couple of cards and have the males begin showing off their best colors and finnage. When kept in constant sight of each other, the males will become so habituated that they

A pair of bettas courting under their bubble nest.

Male bettas show amazing colors when breeding.

almost never display. In order to give the males exercise, betta breeders often shuffle their jarred males, breaking up the habituated neighbors and causing them to start displaying to the new ones. So, if you want to see your males displaying, it's best to keep them out of sight of each other. If you have them lined up where they can see each other, they will display infrequently after an initial bout of showing off.

Breeding

Humans raising bettas obviously rely on their own choices of fish-breeding partners rather than allowing natural selection to take place, so battles between males are not part of a breeding program, but, of course, it is necessary to keep a male and a female together in order to get a spawn. In almost all cases, the two fish are brought together only until a clutch is in the nest, at which point the female is removed. Only very few breeders use a more natural method—keeping the sexes together over prolonged periods. Both approaches require strategies for managing the natural aggression of male bettas, and both are covered in detail in Chapter 7.

Chapter 6

Who Am I?

This retiring little fish is known in its native Thailand as *pla kat* or "biting fish." Common in swamps, canals, and rice paddies it has been bred for sport for centuries. At least three types were bred and raised: *plakat mhor*, the fighting wild-type fish, *plakat cheen*, the long-finned ornamental fish, and *plakat khmer*, the Cambodian variety with colored fins (usually red) and pink or white colorless bodies.

In an effort to produce the perfect fighting fish, various types were cross bred: bred to wild-caught fish: and hybridized with other species such as *Betta smaragdina* and *Betta imbellis*. The end result has been a plethora of modern betta types as well as various fighting types.

Plakat Thai

In recent years the plakat betta, similar to the wild fish in form and finnage but showing increasingly ornamental coloration, has become very popular. Especially beautiful are the fish with metallic colors and descriptive names like "copper" and "platinum."

There are many names for various types of fighting and ornamental Thai varieties, but English speakers generally apply "plakat" to all short-finned bettas. It seems poetically just that after so many years of fancy betta breeding, the original short-finned varieties are getting their own spotlight.

Modern Fancy Bettas

Although wild *Betta splendens* are pretty fish, domesticated strains are vastly different, both in coloration and in finnage. Because the wild betta has red, blue, and green coloration, it has been possible to selectively breed

Generally speaking, the plakat betta is a term used to describe any short-finned betta type.

Crown Tails

The newest fin mutation, crown tails, was an instant hit with aquarists. Bettas with crown tails are currently being developed in some spectacular strains.

the fish in just about any color. In addition, hybrids between *Betta splendens* and related species have increased the variability, especially in a series of metallic colorations that have to be seen to be believed. When you combine color and fin types, there are more than 20,000 possible varieties of bettas!

The genetics of bettas is a fascinating topic. It has been studied extensively, since many breeders find it necessary to learn all about bettas. We will bypass most of this information and just focus on the various colors and how they come to be. If you get into betta breeding seriously, you will probably want to learn more about how these different colors are inherited.

It is important to keep in mind that the various colors interact, and that, generally, pigments in one layer mask other pigments below it. For example, in order to get a pure red fish, there must be reduced black pigment, or the red will not be visible. Below is a very brief introduction to the extremely complex topic of color in bettas.

The Whole Rainbow

Color in bettas is a four-level affair. Their scales are actually transparent, and the visible coloration is caused by pigments in four layers of the skin. Mutations in the genes that control these pigments have resulted in a variety of traits in domesticated bettas.

Yellow Pigment

The deepest and least visible level is the yellow one. This level is significant only when all other pigments are absent. Although the genetics is not yet understood, there are yellow bettas as well as bettas known as "cellophane," that seem to lack most or all of their yellow pigment.

Red Pigment

Next is the red level. The distribution of red at this level is governed by several mutations. Well-bred red bettas are a solid cherry red with no iridescence or other colors in body and fins. Specific genes that influence this level produce traits of red, non-red, extended red, red loss, and red marble. The only one not self-evident is red loss, in which red coloration disappears as the fish matures.

Black Pigment

Then comes the black or "melano" level. Several genes control the presence and distribution of black or brown pigment. Pure black bettas are highly desired, but their breeding is complicated by several factors, not the least of which is the sterility of most black females. Mutations associated with this level are: Cambodian, which restricts color to the fins; blond, which reduces the intensity of black pigment; melano, which increases the intensity of black pigment; and marble. A common effect of melano-producing gene is the "pineapple" pattern of black reticulation around each scale.

Iridescent Pigment

Last is the iridescent level. Crystalline pigments refract light to produce blue and green coloration. Since these are not blue or green pigments per se, the colors can shimmer or change as the fish moves around under a light source. The difficulty in producing true green bettas comes from the fact that a green appearance is determined by a precise combination of factors, not a specific pigment. Mutations which cause the reflective crystals to spread out produce colors such as turquoise, cornflower blue, steel blue, and blue marble.

Interactions

Other genetic factors, such as opaque, which adds a milky overlay, and butterfly, which causes two-toned fins, also affect color in bettas, and all the possible interactions of all the colors produce an enormous variety of color results: chocolate, orange, lavender, and the list goes on and on. It is not an exaggeration to say that it is possible to have a betta in any color of the rainbow.

Fun With Fins

In case thousands of color combinations are not enough for you, bettas also have a great variety of fin types, with new forms and refinements appearing all the time. Bettas of any tail type can be bred in any color.

Round Tail

The round tail is the wild betta type and is found in plakat strains. Various mutations of this gene have been developed into strains of their own.

Veil Tail

The first domesticated fin type, this one was already established when

bettas were first exported from Thailand. All the fins are lengthened in the male, with a long tail that droops behind him.

Delta Tail

Although it's been around for a long time, the genetics for this trait have not been worked out, and it is difficult to breed perfect specimens. The tail is triangular, like a delta guppy's tail. The V-shape gives it the name delta, like the Greek letter.

Double Tail

This fin mutation results in a completely double tail, with two caudal peduncles and two separate tail fins. There are also modifications to the dorsal fin, including additional rays. The double effect is enhanced by the fact that the dorsal and anal fins are approximately the same size and shape.

There are many imperfect variations of this trait, including "heart tails" in which the caudal fins are partially fused, giving a heart shape; fused fins, in which dorsal, caudal, and anal fins are all fused into one; and triple tails. Breeding a perfect double tail, with completely symmetrical tails, is a real challenge. Double tails are manifested in the female as well as the male.

Halfmoon Tail

The ideal here is a full 180-degree spread to the tail. Imagine a delta tail opened up until both edges are straight and vertical, perpendicular to the caudal peduncle—that is the perfect halfmoon. Increased branching of the fin rays produces this effect. Many specimens have considerably less than 180 degrees of spread and are intermediate between halfmoons and deltas. Specimens with a spread of more than 180 degrees are called OHM—over half moon.

Comb & Crown Tails

The comb tail has single ray extensions around the outer edge of the tail that extend beyond the webbing, giving a comb-like appearance. Asian betta breeders first produced crown tails at the end of the twentieth century. This trait affects all the fins, producing long extensions, but in the tail the desired effect is branched ray extensions, at least double, but sometimes triple or quadruple. The rays also extend much farther than in the comb tail, and the tail is described as crown-like.

Don't Mix Males!

Male bettas should never be placed together. In a small container, the resultant combat can seriously injure or kill the fish. If you wish to watch two males flare and show off to each other, simply place their bowls next to each other—they will huff and puff through the glass without any harm.

We are just beginning to see the refinement of this trait, especially as crown tails are being crossed with other tail types. Females also show this trait.

This is a beautiful example of a crown tail betta.

While the wild bettas are not nearly as colorful as their captive-bred counterparts, they are still quite attractive compared to many other wild fishes.

"Wild Bettas"

Many aquarists specialize in what are known as "wild bettas," not indicating *Betta splendens* found in the wild, but species other than *B. splendens*. A few of these have been bred in captivity, but only very recently. You've already seen that *B. smaragdina* and *B. imbellis* have been used in domesticated betta breeding, and those two species have been occasionally available in the hobby for some time. There are, however, a few dozen other species, with more still being discovered. Dedicated aquarists make trips to the Orient to search out wild bettas and bring them back, and specialty importers often make them available.

Most of these fish are drab compared to the common betta, and many come from rainforest streams rather than lowland plains. They prefer cooler water than regular bettas. Many of them are mouthbrooders—instead of making a bubblenest, the male takes all the eggs up into his mouth and broods them in his throat until they are freeswimming.

These species tend to be very expensive, and many have very specific water requirements. As more aquarists have success in breeding these fish in the future, they should become more available and more adaptable.

The Betta Gallery

Betta Bellica

Betta Burdigala

Betta Edithae

Betta Foerschi

Betta Fusca

Betta Imbellis

Betta Macrostoma

Betta Persephone

Betta Smaragdina

Betta splendens

Betta splendens

Betta splendens

Betta M. Eiern

Betta splendens

Chapter 7

Breeding Bettas

Bettas are extremely easy to breed, and though raising their fry is a bit more of a challenge, it is easily within reach of most hobbyists. The most crucial thing to keep in mind when deciding whether or not you want to undertake a betta-spawning project is that a spawn can easily have a few hundred fry, and every single male will need to be isolated in its own container as the babies mature.

It is sometimes possible to raise a group of bettas in a heavily planted pool or pond of several hundred gallons or more, but only a limited number of males can be produced this way, and they are all likely to have tattered fins from the frequent skirmishes that will still take place. But we're getting ahead of ourselves. Let's look at the steps you will need to follow to successfully breed bettas.

Selecting a Pair

Obviously a primary concern when breeding bettas is obtaining a good pair. Not only do the male and female both have to be healthy and demonstrate traits appropriate to their strain, they have to be genetically compatible so that the spawn will look as good as or better than their parents.

Getting a Female

Obtaining a male betta is very easy; almost any fish retailer will have a selection. Finding a female is much harder, finding a good one is harder still, and finding a good one that will make a good match for your male is even harder. Because they are so much less colorful in most cases, and because their finnage is much less elaborate in all cases, female bettas are not regularly stocked by retailers. In addition, many "females" turn out to be immature males that are mistaken for females, and once you get them home, their fins grow out, and you discover the error.

Female bettas are available through your local pet shop or specialized betta breeders throughout the world.

It's easier to judge the genetic makeup of a male betta, since the females often don't manifest their color or fin potential.

A female betta's genetics is not always discernible. Traits like Cambodian and double tail will be obvious, but the subtleties of color and finnage may not be. For example, crown-tail females show fin extensions, but it is hard to judge the extent of expression of the trait, and therefore it is difficult to assess her as a breeder. Males are much easier to judge, since they show full expression of their traits.

What About the Male?

Plenty of breeder-worthy male bettas can be found at pet shops, but if you are searching for really special colors or varieties, then it is usually best to get the male from a betta breeder as well. It takes the same expense and effort to breed top specimens as it does to breed fish of lesser quality, so it makes sense to spend the little extra needed to obtain a pair of quality fish.

Buying From a Betta Breeder

Buying from betta breeders is in most cases the best way to get a female betta. Not only do they have plenty of them to choose from, but they will know the lineage of the female and have a good idea of what her genetic makeup is.

Bettas are not overly difficult to breed as long as their basic requirements are met.

72

Bettas

It is important to say that pet shops bettas are not usually of poor quality—they make great pets, but they are not usually prime breeding specimens. People who just want a beautiful fish often do not care if its fins or colors do not conform perfectly to the standards by which bettas are shown and judged, so a breeder's culls, which are perfectly sound and healthy but simply lack the desired conformation, are sold by retailers for much less money than is commanded by the top few specimens reserved as breeders.

Better Betta Breeding

Although breeders do make test pairings, just to see what they get, most pairings are based on genetic compatibility. It is therefore usually preferable to buy breeding stock directly from a betta breeder. Not only can the breeder help you choose which strain and which fish you should work with, he or she can provide you with a pair that has compatible genetics. Certain traits will mask other

Lighting

Bettas prefer low light levels, and they need very little light for successful spawning. Any light sufficient for your needs will be fine for your fish. If you use live plants in your spawning setups, you will, of course, need adequate light for the species used.

The male will catch each egg as it falls from the female and place it in the bubblenest.

traits, and sometimes the traits of both parents will not be apparent in the offspring. A basic knowledge of betta genetics can help prevent these disappointments.

Breeding Facts & Superstitions

Aquarists are often guilty of superstitious behavior. Someone follows presumed good advice and puts a teaspoon of salt per 5 gallons (19 l) of water in his tanks, and his fish do well, so he always puts in the salt. He never considers that his fish would have done as well—or even better—without the salt.

Well, there are quite a few traditions in betta breeding that simply do not hold up to experimental investigation. You will hear such recommendations quite often, but experienced breeders have found they are be quite unnecessary. Here are the major factors in setting up a betta breeding tank, with myths identified where they exist.

Water Volume

The facts that wild bettas will spawn in a flooded hoofprint, or that captive fish have spawned successfully in quart jars, have led some people to assume they need confined spaces. Tests indicate that bettas spawn most readily in volumes between 2 and 10 gallons (8 and 40 liters), but these tests do not parse out all the factors involved. For example, spawning readiness is the single most crucial factor, and two absolutely ready fish will spawn successfully whether tossed together into a small jar or into a rice paddy. Providing sufficient room for one of the pair to escape the other's advances enables them both to come to spawning readiness without coming to harm. In addition, poor water conditions diminish spawning success, and water conditions in larger volumes is much more stable.

Water Temperature

Although bettas may breed at a wide range of temperatures, they are most likely to spawn when kept warm, near but not more than 84°F (29°C) Much above this limit, the fish will be reluctant to spawn, and any fry produced will be weak and unlikely to survive.

Conditioning the Adults

Conditioning is the key to successful spawnings. Proper care will usually condition bettas quite well, but a little extra live food always works wonders.

Always be sure to have a tight-fitting cover on your betta's tank or bowl.

Water Level

As we've noted, wild bettas often spawn in extremely shallow water, and low water level is often said to be necessary for breeding these fish. The danger to fry falling to the bottom is typically cited. Many breeders, however, find no difference in success with water levels from 3 to 12 in. (7.5 to 30 cm), and they report that even when fry are not returned to the nest by their father, they will survive on the bottom until they are freeswimming.

Tank Cover

Keeping the spawning/rearing tank well covered, is, however, something that makes a big difference in many cases. When the aquarium is tightly covered, the air above the water remains warm and humid, just like the air in the betta's steamy natural habitat. Air that is cool or dry will harm the bubblenest and the fry. This is especially important when the fry are a few weeks old and are developing their labyrinth organs. If the aquarium is in a fishroom, the air will generally be warm and moist enough; otherwise, the tank should be kept covered at all times.

Aeration & Filtration

Aeration and filtration, though recommended for bettas in bowls or in tanks, are generally not recommended in the betta breeding tank. Water movement disrupts the nest and overwhelms the fry, which are adapted to absolutely still water environments.

The male should be separated from the female until she is conditioned for spawning.

Some betta breeders, however make use of the special properties of sponge filters in their breeding tanks. By adjusting the uplift tube of an air-driven sponge filter so that it is above the surface of the water, you will produce a very gentle bubbling that will cause virtually no water movement while still providing biofiltration. In addition, the suction will be so minimal that it will not draw new fry into the sponge; in fact, freeswimming fry will soon be found grazing on the multitude of microorganisms that typically colonize a sponge filter.

Separating the Pair

If you put a male that is ready to spawn and a ripe female together, they may get right to spawning with no aggression at all. Usually, however, there is a certain amount of sparring, and when one of the fish is not ready to spawn but the other is, there can be serious injury, and one may kill the other. Although most often the male will kill the female, the reverse can happen.

Various methods are used to separate the prospective mates, both physical and visual. Visual barriers can be plants (live or plastic), driftwood, rocks, plastic pipe, or any other insoluble objects. Typically these afford sufficient protection, and

A male Shortfin fighter stands guard over his newly hatched fry.

when both fish are ready to spawn, they're available to each other.

Physical barriers include partitions and various strategies such as floating the female in a livebearer breeding trap in the male's tank. When the pair's behavior indicates they are ready, the female is tipped into the tank. Many breeders rely on the female's desire to join the male and use a small plastic cup for her floating home so that when she is ready she can just jump out and join him.

The Spawning

The breeding behavior of all fishes is variable, but bettas are more variable than many other species. On the other hand, people's accounts of betta spawning are often quite rigid, claiming this or that does or does not happen. This can be very confusing, especially if your spawning bettas do not follow a particular pattern. Let's look at the components of a successful spawn and how they come together.

The Bubblenest

Building a bubblenest is a major part of a male betta's behavioral repertoire. Betta breeders have observed young males barely two months old, just newly in jars, frothing them up. Nests in jars are indicators of good, healthy fish. Bettas

Female bettas may need a longer conditioning time compared to males, so patience is important in this process.

Bettas

in need of a change of water lose interest in nest building, and a change of water stimulates nest building.

Also, when strange males are placed next to each other in their respective jars, this seems to stimulate nest building. After an initial period of aggressive displays, one or both will usually settle down and build a nest. Some breeders take advantage of this, rearranging the jars occasionally to get the fish to exercise.

A similar response is seen when strange females are placed next to the male. Normally, once a female is in sight, a healthy male will start to construct a bubble-nest either using bubbles alone or

incorporating floating plants if they are available.

The male betta's bubblenest is a vital and distinctive part of the spawning process, but males vary greatly on the details. Many will build a bubblenest even when kept alone, others start blowing bubbles when they see another

Bubblenests may be built under floating pieces of foam in an aquarium.

betta, and still others wait until they meet up with a receptive female before starting the nest.

Male bettas take great pride in their bubblenests.

Some nests are loose and scattered, while others are dense, rising an inch (2.5 cm) or more out of the water. Large nests may almost cover the surface of the tank, while small ones may be tucked away tightly in a corner. Some males will build virtually no nest at all and still be successful. A male might just ball up the eggs in a mass with no conventional nest. Another will build a nest covering a considerable amount of water-surface area, while yet another will be content with a much smaller nest of considerable thickness. Also, one male will start building a nest at the sight of a female and another only when he has actually spawned with a female.

The male may continue to build a nest even through and during a spawning, and keep it up while the eggs are developing. Often he will start to enlarge the nest as the eggs hatch and as the young begin to move away from the central area of the nest.

Eggs sometimes are pushed well up into the bubbles of a nest so that it is difficult to see them, while other times the eggs are clumped together just under the nest bottom.

Nest Building At its Best!

We find that maximum nest-building behavior occurs when the barometer is changing rapidly. The temperature of the water is a great stimulator of nest building as well, with 84°F (27°C) considered ideal, though fish have been known to build nests at all temperatures from 64° to 86°F (18° to 29°C).

water plants found floating in natural betta habitats in Thailand.

While the bubblenest, the shallow water, and the father's ferocity protect the eggs from predation, they place the male at risk, especially from birds. Building the nest under a floating leaf will hide the male's activities from aerial predators.

Bubblenests are commonly built under floating plant material.

Many breeders find that something floating will soon have a nest built under it—things such as a floating plant like water sprite, Amazon swordplant, or even lettuce. Others use a piece of wax paper or plastic food wrapper and even bottoms of plastic cups or plastic lids of various kinds.

University investigations have shown that males prefer something that is round, about the diameter of a grapefruit, and yellow in color as a floating anchor for their nests. These characteristics correspond with dead leaves of the

Courtship

When a well-conditioned pair discover each other, there is usually instant communication. They spread their fins and gills, and their colors brighten. The female, who normally sports horizontal stripes or no pattern, takes on a vertical barring. The fish

The spawning process begins with the male pursuing the female and even trying nip at her fins.

swim side-by-side, trembling and perhaps even slapping at each other. They may separate, but soon come back together.

Soon the male becomes more aggressive, slapping the female and lunging at her, biting and nipping. If the female is ready to spawn, she dodges these attacks but quickly returns. Typically she will go hide from time to time, and then the male works on his bubblenest. The female will then reappear, and the ritual is repeated. Brilliant displays of color and aggression are part of the courting ritual.

Often the male is actively engaged in nest building when he is not chasing the female, and within a short time he will stop chasing and start trying to lure the female to the nest. He presents a side view, with fins and gills spread, wagging his body back and forth in an S, then swimming back to the nest. She follows a bit, then breaks off, and it can take some time for the male to lure her all the way to the nest.

Finally the female will approach the male under the nest and show her readiness by swimming toward him in a head-downward

position, fins clamped, and with a shimmy or snakelike swim pattern. Her ovipositor is visible as a small tube protruding from her vent.

This submissive approach gentles the male. The pair circles, nosing each other's sides, and eventually winds up with the female upside down, the male on his side, curved over her body. This embrace position places their vents in proximity, and the fish freeze for a moment. The first embraces are usually dry runs, but soon they will produce from a few to 50 or more eggs.

The male usually recovers from the embrace first and heads down to retrieve the eggs in his mouth and blow them up into the nest. When he releases the female, she floats toward the surface on her side, seemingly in a

81

Brilliant displays of color and aggression are part of the courting ritual.

The male gently embraces the female as the actual mating begins.

trance. She recovers slowly, then rights herself and often assists in egg gathering.

When the female has no more eggs, she retreats, and the male tends the nest. At this point most breeders remove the female. The male mouths the eggs, pushes them up among the bubbles, and repairs and enlarges the nest. He sometimes will build another nest and move the eggs to it.

The eggs hatch in about 24 hours, but the fry hang tail-down in the nest for another 36 hours. After that they gradually take on a horizontal swimming position and begin to wander from the nest area. The male keeps watch and does all he can to corral the fry in the nest area. Many breeders remove the male at this point and leave the fry on their own.

Raising the Fry

The key to raising betta fry is the same as with almost any other fish—balancing the need for copious food with the need for clean water. Nothing

soria, microworms, vinegar eels, and other smaller-than-baby-brine-shrimp foods. Other very successful breeders, however, do not bother with these but start with baby brine shrimp right away. They report that even fry too small to swallow shrimp nauplii whole will tear them to pieces and eat them.

How is this possible? Well, first of all, different strains of bettas may have different sized fry. There are probably also trade-offs, such as the few fry in a batch that starve to death because they cannot feed on brine shrimp are offset by the few fry in another batch that cannot eat enough microorganisms to satisfy their needs. Most likely the principal factor is simply that there are many ways to properly feed newborn bettas.

Another factor to consider is that many spawning tanks are swarming with microorganisms that betta fry can

invites stunting, disease, and mortality faster than water polluted with decomposing food. Since heavy filtration is not an option with bettas, breeders use frequent water changes to keep things clean.

First Foods

Much betta literature is devoted to the need for micro foods for newly hatched fry, and many betta breeders use infu-

As the eggs fall from the female, the male gently picks them up and places them in the bubblenest.

The spawning ritual is often described as a beautiful dance between the male and female bettas.

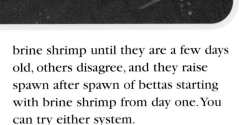

After approximately 24 hours, the fry begin to hatch and hang tail down from the bubble nest for another 36 hours until they become freeswimming.

feed on. Any aquarium houses many of these tiny creatures, but live plants increase the populations, and sponge filters are full of them. The use of plants and sponge filters in a betta spawning tank ensures the presence of micro foods for the fry, even if none are intentionally added.

So, although many breeders will insist that betta fry cannot handle baby

SMALL FRY

The Miracle of Life

Raising a betta spawn can be a wonderful introduction for a child to the marvels of life. The courtship and spawning of bettas is fascinating, and the fry grow quickly from tiny slivers barely visible in the nest to full-sizes adults. Every day brings new wonders and discoveries.

brine shrimp until they are a few days old, others disagree, and they raise spawn after spawn of bettas starting with brine shrimp from day one. You can try either system.

In any case, soon the fry will be gorging themselves on baby shrimp. It is important to keep their little bellies pink and plump—a magnifying glass will help you check on them. It is vital that you siphon the bottom of the tank every day to remove all detritus, and remove a good portion of the old water at the same time. Replace the water with conditioned water of the same temperature. Such a regimen provides ample food for rapid growth while maintaining water purity, which is even more important for fry than for adult bettas.

Growout Tanks

The aquarium for raising the fry should be covered to maintain heat and humidity in the airspace to protect the developing labyrinth organs. Gentle filtration is good—air-driven box filters or sponge filters are excellent. As they get bigger, the baby bettas will be able to handle larger foods, and soon they will be eating the same foods as their parents.

Since many bettas are spawned in small containers, and since many betta spawns number in the hundreds—with a spawn of 1000 occasionally reported —moving the fry to larger quarters is something that will be necessary, probably sooner rather than later. Although they start out quite tiny, bettas grow rapidly, but if crowded they will not grow properly. Most

The Expert Knows

Brine Shrimp Culture

Newly hatched brine shrimp have been the staple of fish breeding for over a century. Today they are starting to be replaced by manufactured alternatives, but for many aquarists, the brine shrimp hatcher is the foundational piece of equipment of the fishroom. There are many resources in books and online from which you can learn the best methods of producing this time-honored food for baby fishes.

breeders figure on about 10 fry per gallon in the growout tanks, but this is possible only with very frequent, large water changes.

If properly fed and kept in clean water, the fry will be sexually distinguishable at about two months of age. As the males develop longer fins and begin squabbling, move them to individual accommodations. Females can be left together in the tank. By the time they reach three months, you should be able to see which have the traits

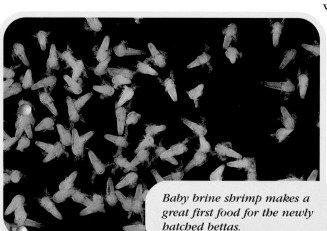

Baby brine shrimp makes a great first food for the newly hatched bettas.

After a few months of age, the young bettas will be sexually dimorphic and males and females can be easily separated from each other.

you bred for, and you can begin to select the next generation of breeding stock.

"Natural" Breeding

Betta breeders typically use the system outlined above, one pair per tank, removing the female after spawning and the male when the fry become freeswimming. This is probably the best way to get the maximum number of fry in the least time, but some aquarists have had success with more natural setups.

These range from keeping one or more females with a male in a large aquarium to maintaining a group of mixed sexes in a very large tank or pond. In all cases heavy plant thickets provide refuge for targets of aggression, whether male or female, and sanctuary for fry.

It is not uncommon for a male to tend several spawns in his nest. These can be from a single female or various mates. As the fry grow, they move away from the nest, and if there is sufficient plant cover, many of them will survive. It is, therefore, possible to keep a pair or trio of bettas in a large planted tank, removing fry from the floating plants from time to time. The only concern would be proper feeding of the fry, though with the right care, there will soon be bettas of all ages coexisting. As males begin to mature, however, they would definitely have to be removed.

When a sufficiently large aquarium is used, it is even possible to maintain a breeding colony with more than one male. The most common example of such a setup is an outdoor pond. Putting several male and even more female bettas in to a well-planted pond for the summer will often result in a considerable harvest of bettas a few months later.

The major drawback of these natural breeding groups is the lack of control. Fry cannot be raised intensively, since they are always in the presence of adults. There is also no control of breedings; with two or more females, there is no way to know which fry belong to which, and when there are two or more males, it is even more disorganized. Nevertheless, the process is much more relaxed for the caretaker, and it works for some fanciers.

Some hobbyists prefer to house bettas in aquariums that are planted, thus providing a more natural approach to betta breeding.

Java fern can provide the perfect anchor for a bubble nest.

Bettas & Beyond

There are many ways in which people grow in the betta hobby after their initial pet betta or two. The first, and most common—breeding, was actually already covered in the last chapter. Betta clubs and betta shows are also popular.

Betta Organizations & Clubs

People with similar interests enjoy getting together, and betta fanciers are no exception. Many betta keepers join local aquarium clubs, but in some places there are so many betta fans that they have created specifically betta clubs in their locality. These groups meet regularly and typically have a speaker who gives a presentation on some topic of interest to the membership; this is then often followed by raffles, auctions, and refreshments. Many have regular shows as well, where members can bring in their prize specimens to pit against other members' fish.

Join a Club!

Joining an aquarium club, whether a general group or a betta club, is one of the best ways to be more involved in your hobby and to enjoy it better.

Obtaining Quality Stock

Aside from bringing betta keepers together, clubs provide excellent opportunities for fanciers to obtain quality stock from each other. Along with great bettas, members are able to get great advice from experienced betta enthusiasts. Their help and

Fellow club members are a great source for high-quality bettas.

SMALL FRY

A Lifetime Hobby

Many betta breeders began keeping bettas when they were children, and all types of aquarists often enjoy the hobby for life. Keeping fish is educational and fun, and it is active, engaging mind and body as opposed to staring at a screen and clicking a mouse.

support are invaluable to newcomers to the betta fancy.

In the last chapter we also discussed getting quality breeding stock from breeders or specialized stores rather than from regular pet shops. But other than from each other, where do the breeders get their stock?

In the case of bettas, the answer most often is from Asia. Many factors contribute to the superiority of bettas from Asian breeders. These include the historical factor—Asian aquarists have a big head start on us—but also the fact that raising any aquarium species is easier there, and raising bettas is even easier by far.

A breeder in Southeast Asia can take advantage of less expensive labor, readily available live foods, and a climate that permits either indoor or outdoor setups. They can maintain rack upon rack of betta jars, changing the water completely every day and conditioning their fish with the best foods, all with minimal expense.

Blackworms can be expensive to buy unless bulk orders are placed.

Of course, you cannot simply contact an Asian fish farmer and order a pair or two of bettas. Betta clubs make it possible to import wholesale lots of bettas from the Orient. While minimum orders and transportation expenses make it impractical for individual betta keepers to import these quality fish, club members can pool their orders and divide up the fish when they arrive.

Blackworms

Many aquarists, including lots of betta fanciers, love to feed blackworms to their fish for the simple reason that they obviously love eating them.

Nothing will bring a fish into breeding condition faster than live foods, and blackworms will do the trick nicely. What does this have to do with betta clubs?

Well, although a few people cultivate blackworms at home, most rely on buying this excellent fish food, and this works well for feeding a few bettas. But for a fishroom with hundreds of bettas in it, this isn't practical…unless you buy the worms

Fishrooms

Aquarists who expand in their hobby often wind up with a fishroom. The peculiarities of a betta fancier's fishroom are based on the need to isolate all those males. Racks of jars or other setups are prominent, and unless a flow-through system is used, changing jar water is the primary chore.

Betta shows are a great place to gather, meet new betta fanciers, and see bettas like this one!

National & International Organizations

The next step would be to join a national or international betta organization. One of the important functions of these organizations is to sanction local shows. For many people, breeding bettas to an accepted standard of perfection and competing in betta shows is all part of the enjoyment.

Showing bettas is closely tied to breeding them, since the real reward comes when a fish you have bred and raised wins. Attending betta shows, however, is enjoyable whether or not you are into showing your fish. Nowhere else can you see such a variety of superb animals in one place. New variants and refinements are often first made public at national or international shows. Often high-quality breeding stock is available for sale at these shows, which makes them a great place for you to get your start in commercial betta breeding.

in bulk. Even still, the freight on worms from growers who raise them in farms full of ponds—often in California—can be more than the cost of the worms themselves.

As with imported fish, however, club members can pool their blackworm orders and have them shipped quite economically, especially when figured on a per-pound basis.

Hands-on Experience

Club members love to visit each other's fishrooms, and one way newbies can learn is by helping out a fellow club member. An afternoon helping a breeder change water in his growout jars and chatting about bettas is better than an armful of books for teaching proper betta husbandry.

Sharing the Passion

Attending conventions and shows gives you the chance to mingle with like-minded people who share your passion for bettas.

Resources

Magazines

Tropical Fish Hobbyist
1 T.F.H. Plaza
3rd & Union Avenues
Neptune City, NJ 07753
Phone: (732) 988-8400
E-mail: info@tfh.com
www.tfhmagazine.com

Internet Resources

A World of Fish
www.aworldoffish.com

Advanced Bettas
http://groups.msn.com/AdvancedBettas

Aquarium Hobbyist
www.aquariumhobbyist.com

Betta Webring
www.bettasrus.com

Delphi Betta Forum
http://forums.delphiforums.com/bettabreeders

FINS: The Fish Information Service
http://fins.actwin.com

Fish Geeks
www.fishgeeks.com

Fish Index
www.fishindex.com

MyFishTank.Net
www.myfishtank.net

New York Area Bettas
www.babb.info

Tropical Resources
www.tropicalresources.net

Associations & Societies

California Betta Society
An active IBC chapter on the Pacific Coast.
http://cbs.bettas.org

Association of Aquarists
David Davis, Membership Secretary
2 Telephone Road
Portsmouth, Hants, England
PO4 0AY
Phone: 01705 798686

**Canadian Association of
Aquarium Clubs**
Miecia Burden, Membership
Coordinator
142 Stonehenge Pl.
Kitchener, Ontario, Canada
N2N 2M7
Phone: (517) 745-1452
E-mail: mbburden@look.ca
www.caoac.on.ca

Canadian Bettas
If you are in Canada, the IBC chapter
for you is Betta Breeders Canada.
http://groups.yahoo.com/group/BBCanada

Bettas

Federation of American Aquarium Societies
Jane Benes, Secretary
923 Wadsworth Street
Syracuse, NY 13208-2419
Phone: (513) 894-7289
E-mail: jbenes01@yahoo.com
www.gcca.net/faas

International Betta Congress
Steve Van Camp, Secretary
923 Wadsworth St.
Syracuse, NY 13208
Phone: (315) 454-4792
E-mail: bettacongress@yahoo.com
www.ibcbettas.com

National Aquarium in Baltimore
501 E. Pratt Street
Baltimore, Maryland, 21202.
410-576-3800 (daily 9:00 a.m. to 4:30 p.m.)
www.aqua.org

Resources

Glossary: Bettas

betta: technically any fish of the genus *Betta*, but usually a *Betta splendens*. Also **Siamese fighting fish**.

betta barracks: a setup with multiple compartments for maintaining individual male bettas while permitting water flow through the setup.

betta bowl: a bowl meant to house a betta; often such a setup is sorely lacking as a betta habitat, particularly in terms of temperature and water quality.

betta vase: a vase housing a betta with a live plant whose roots dangle in the water with the fish. Fine in concept, a betta vase is often deficient in implementation. See **betta bowl.**

bubblenest: a nest made by a male betta by blowing bubbles and sometimes incorporating bits of plant material. During spawning the fertilized eggs are spat up into the nest by the male, and he tends the newly hatched fry in the nest until they become free swimming.

butterfly: a variety of betta in which the body color extends partway into the fins, after which the fins are clear.

Cambodian: a betta color pattern of a colorless (and therefore pink) body and colored fins. The fins are often red but may be other colors as well.

cellophane: a betta completely lacking in color pigment. The eye, however, is dark, so this is not an albino.

combtail: a betta with extended rays in the fins, giving a comb-like appearance.

crowntail (CT): a betta with greatly extended (and often divided) rays in the fins, producing the crown-like pattern.

double tail (DT): a betta with two complete tails, including a double peduncle.

half moon (HM): a betta with a tail making a 180-degree spread.

melano: the betta gene for black pigment, part of black and steel colorations. Melano females are often sterile.

over half moon (OHM): a betta with a tail making a greater than 180-degree spread.

plakat: The Thai name for a betta, meaning "biting fish." Usually used to refer to short-finned betta varieties. Also **pla kat**.

roundtail: the wild type tail.

spawning embrace: the wrapping of the male betta around the female at the time of her expelling eggs and his fertilizing them, after which the fish appear to go into a momentary trance. The embrace is repeated many times during a spawning.

Siamese fighting fish: a Betta splendens.

Wild betta: besides referring to wild-caught Betta splendens, this term is used to refer to the species of the genus Betta which do not have domesticated varieties. Many of these species are mouthbrooders.

Glossary: General Aquariums

acid water: water with more hydrogen ions than hydroxyl ions, i.e., water with a pH below 7.0.

adipose fin: a small fleshy fin without spines behind the dorsal and present on some fishes.

aeration: agitation or other water movement that facilitates the inputting of oxygen and removal of carbon dioxide from aquarium water. Both air and water pumps can be used to aerate an aquarium. It is the movement of the water, not the air bubbles, that accomplishes the aeration. See **gas exchange, oxygenation.**

aerobic: occurring in the presence of oxygen.

airstone: a porous device, often ceramic but sometimes of wood, that releases a stream of air bubbles into the aquarium when attached to an air pump.

algae: this non-technical term refers to a wide variety of photosynthetic organisms, both prokaryotes and eukaryotes, including single-celled creatures like cyanobacteria, diatoms, and dinoflagellates as well as multicellular red, brown, and green seaweeds such as kelp. "Algae" is plural; the singular is "alga."

alkalinity: the buffering capacity of water that resists acidification, depending mostly on dissolved carbonates and bicarbonates. Water with low alkalinity can experience rapid and dangerous drops in pH. Sometimes misleadingly called "carbonate hardness."

anal fin: the single fin posterior to the fish's vent. Also the **ventral fin.**

anerobic: occurring in the absence of oxygen.

anoxic: occurring in the presence of extremely low levels of oxygen.

aquarium: technically any container used to hold water for keeping fish, but usually made of five panels of glass in a rectangular prism.

basic water: water with more hydroxyl ions than hydrogen ions, i.e., water with a pH above 7.0.

BBS: acronym for baby brine shrimp.

biofiltration: the use of bacterial colonies to remove toxic ammonia and nitrite from aquarium water. A biofilter must be carefully nurtured when an aquarium is first set up. (See **cycling.**)

blackworms: small aquatic worms widely used as live food for aquarium fish.

brackish: water with measurable salinity, but less salty than seawater; occurs naturally wherever freshwater rivers meet the ocean.

brine shrimp: crustaceans of the genus *Artemia* that live in hypersaline habitats. An extremely popular fish food, used live, frozen, and freeze-dried.

canister filter: an aquarium filter that houses media in a canister through which aquarium water is pumped under pressure. This is an extremely efficient filtration method, ideal for large aquaria.

carnivore: a fish whose diet consists primarily of animal material.

caudal fin: the tail fin of a fish.

caudal peduncle: the muscular end of a fish's body to which the tail fin attaches, typically narrower than the rest of the body.

chemical filtration: removing dissolved pollutants from aquarium

water, usually by adsorption into a bed of activated carbon.

crossbreed: to mate fish of one strain with those of another. This is done either to strengthen an inbred strain or to bring in desired traits that are lacking in the strain but present in the other. Also **outcross.**

cycling: establishing the biofilter in a new aquarium. The process involves allowing ammonia to build up to feed nitrifying bacterial colonies, followed by allowing nitrite to build up to feed other colonies, and ending with a mature biofilter.

Daphnia: a genus of freshwater crustaceans that are widely used a food for aquarium fishes. Also known as "water fleas."

delta tail: the ideal delta tail is a perfect triangle, like the Greek letter ?.

denitrification: the anaerobic process in which bacteria convert nitrate to nitrogen gas.

dorsal fin: a fin on a fish's back. Almost all fish have a dorsal fin, some types of fish have two dorsal fins, and a few primitive species have numerous dorsals.

eye spot: a "fake eye" marking of a fish's body or fin, thought to confuse predators into targeting less vital body parts. Also **ocellus**.

101

filter feeder: a fish that feeds by straining water through its gills, retaining any small plants or animals and releasing the water. See **planktonivore**.

filtration: cleansing of aquarium water. See **mechanical filtration, chemical filtration, and biofiltration.**

fry: baby fish, singular or plural: "one fry" or "many fry."

gas exchange: the inputting of oxygen and removal of carbon dioxide from aquarium water through agitation or other water movement. Both air and water pumps can be used to move the water to facilitate gas exchange. See **aeration, oxygenation.**

gills: a fish's organs of respiration, consisting of finely branched, capillary-rich tissue. Breathing forces water over the gills, in the mouth and out the **opercula**. Gas exchange takes place in and some wastes are secreted by the gills.

hard water: water with a high concentration of dissolved minerals, principally calcium and magnesium.

head-and-lateral-line erosion (HLLE): a deterioration of the sensory pits on a fish's head and flanks, which can cause severe damage if untreated. There are several postulated causes, including infection, dietary deficiencies, and poor water quality.

herbivore: a fish whose diet consists primarily of plant material.

hybrid: in a strict sense, an organism whose parents were of different species; sometimes incorrectly used to refer to crossbred animals. Several popular aquarium fish are of hybrid origin, especially livebearers.

ich: sometimes "ick." Whitespot disease, a parasitic infection by the ciliated protozoan *Ichthyophthirius multifiliis*, that encysts on a fish's skin and gills. Potentially lethal, but treatable with salt, heat, chemicals, or a combination of these.

inbreed: to make use of any breeding program that mates close relatives such as father-daughter or brother-sister. It is very useful for fixing traits but in excess it can lead to weak fish and genetic abnormalities.

Infusoria: a term for a multitude of microscopic organisms widely used to feed fry too small to consume BBS.

interspecific: between individuals of different species (e.g., interspecific aggression).

intraspecific: between members of one species (e.g., intraspecific aggression).

labyrinth fish: an anabantoid fish possessing a labyrinth organ, a structure used to extract oxygen from atmospheric air much like a lung.

lateral line: a row of pit-like sensory organs along the side of a fish's body.

linebreed: to breed related fish while avoiding the excesses of strict inbreeding, usually by mating less closely related fish. Often several familial lines of a strain are maintained and occasionally outcrossed to each other.

livebearer: technically any fish that gives birth to live young as opposed to laying eggs, but most commonly referring to the family Poeciliidae.

mechanical filtration: removing suspended debris from aquarium water, usually by passing it through pads of various fibers or foam.

micropredator: a fish that feeds on small organisms like worms and crustaceans.

microworms: non parasitic nematodes that are grown in a cereal-based medium as fish food. Widely used as a substitute or complement for BBS.

mouthbrooding: a reproductive strategy in which the eggs are incubated in a parent fish's throat. After release, the fry may be taken back into the mouth when threatened.

nauplius (pl. nauplii): the free-swimming larval stage of many crustaceans, such as brine shrimp.

nitrification: the aerobic process in which bacteria convert ammonia into nitrite, and then nitrite to nitrate.

ocellus (pl. ocelli): a "fake eye" marking of a fish's body or fin, thought to confuse predators into lunging for less vital body parts. Also **eye spot**.

omnivore: a fish whose diet consists of both plant and animal material.

operculum (pl. opercula): a fish's gill cover. Many fish flare these out perpendicular to their body as part of a threat or courting display.

outcross: to mate fish of one strain with those of another. This is done either to strengthen an inbred strain or to bring in desired traits that are lacking in the strain but present in the other. Also **crossbreed**.

oviparous: reproduction in which the eggs are laid or scattered, then undergo incubation in the aquatic environment. See **ovoviviparous** and **viviparous**.

ovoviviparous: reproduction in which the eggs are retained within the female's body until they hatch, at which time the fry are born. The female, however, does not provide nourishment beyond the egg. See **oviparous** and **viviparous**.

oxygenation: the dissolving of oxygen into water, also by implication the removal of dissolved carbon dioxide from the water. See **gas exchange**.

paired fins: the fins of a fish that come in pairs, one on each side of the body. These include the **pectoral** and **pelvic fins**.

parasite: an organism that depends on the presence of another organism to carry out life functions for it. A parasite usually lives within the body tissues of its host. Many fish diseases are caused by parasites.

pectoral fins: the fins behind the operculum, similar to our arms.

pelvic fins: the fins in front of the anus, similar to our legs.

pH: a logarithmic measurement of how acid or basic water is, for *pondus hydrogeni*. The usual range is 0 to 14, with 7 being defined as neutral. Most fish do well with a pH of between 6 and 8.

pigment: substances which produce a fish's color. A pigment can be either a substance of a particular color or a clear crystal which refracts light to reflect a certain color. Fish often have both types of pigments.

piscivore: a fish whose diet consists primarily of other fishes.

planktonivore: a fish whose diet consists primarily tiny organisms (plankton). See **filter feeder.**

powerhead: a small submersible water pump.

predator: a fish that feeds on other animals.

prey: a fish that is eaten by another animal.

reverse osmosis (RO): a process which uses water pressure to force water through a membrane, leaving most dissolved substances behind. This produces extremely pure water with no hardness or alkalinity; such water is used to mix artificial seawater and as a major component in water mixes for fish that require very soft, very acid environments.

secondary sex characteristics: gender-linked physical traits not part of the reproductive organs, such as sex-dependent coloration or finnage.

soft water: water with a low concentration of dissolved minerals.

substrate: the material on the bottom of an aquarium, typically sand or gravel, but sometimes mud, peat, or other substances.

swim bladder: an sac-like organ in most fishes that is inflated with air or with other gases and that the fish uses to modify its buoyancy in order to move upward or downward in the water. Diseases of the swim bladder manifest in an inability to maintain proper buoyancy—usually with the fish floating helplessly at the surface.

top off: to add water to an aquarium to make up for water lost through evaporation.

undergravel filter (UGF): a filter that uses the gravel bed of the aquarium as its medium. A slotted plate sits under the gravel, with lift tubes through which an airstone or a powerhead draws water down through the gravel bed and up from under the plate. A **reverse-flow UGF** uses a powerhead to pump water down the tubes, under the plate, and up through the gravel bed.

unpaired fins: the fins of a fish that are single and insert into the mid-sagittal plane. These include the caudal, dorsal, and ventral fins.

veiltail: a fish with a tail greatly enlarged compared to the wild type. Usually the other fins are also elongated.

velvet: a parasitic infection by a dinoflagellate in the genus Oodinium. The spots are much smaller than with ich and may be yellowish. This is also a potentially lethal and highly contagious disease, but also treatable with salt, heat, chemicals, or a combination of these.

ventral fin: the single fin posterior to the fish's vent. Also the **anal fin**.

viviparous: reproduction in which the eggs are retained within the female, and the developing young are nourished in some way from the female's body until they are born. See **oviparous** and **ovoviviparous**.

water change: the removal of a volume of water from an aquarium and its replacement with the same volume of clean, fresh water, performed to remove wastes from the aquarium. Water changes are a simple and effective maintenance procedure for all aquaria and should be large and frequent.

Index

About the Author

David E. Boruchowitz has been keeping and raising fishes for more than 50 years. The author of numerous books and articles, he also serves as Editor-in-Chief of *Tropical Fish Hobbyist Magazine*. David lives on a farm in New York State with his family and over a dozen aquariums.

Photo credits

Photos courtesy of TFH archives
Illustration on page 22 courtesy of David Boruchowitz

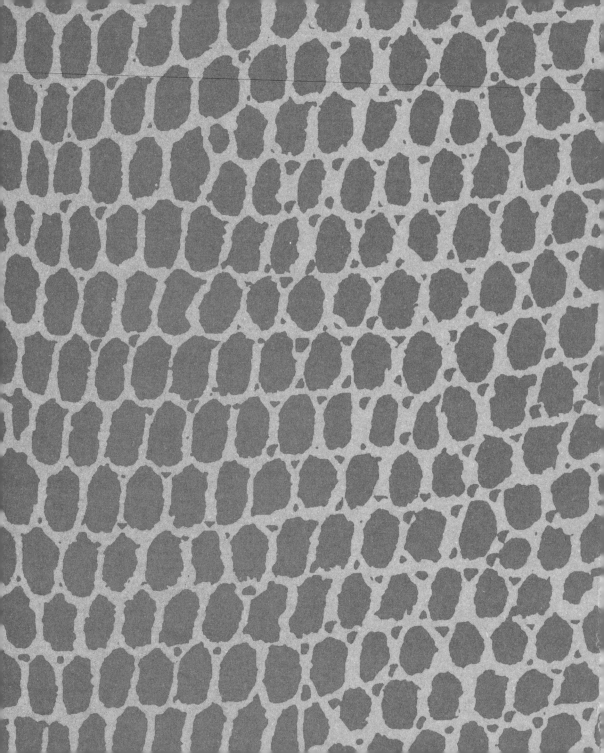